WRITERS AND THEIR WORK NO. 131

Francis Bacon

by J. MAX PATRICK

Published for The British Council
and The National Book League
by Longmans, Green & Co.

Two shillings and sixpence net

This is a tribute paid on the four hundredth anniversary of Bacon's birth in 1561. He is here interpreted as the supreme English exemplar of the Baroque Man.

Professor J. Max Patrick, the son of a Canadian father and an American mother, was born in Washington State, brought up in Canada, and educated at the University of Toronto and at Balliol College, Oxford. After three years as History Master at St. Edward's School, Oxford, he returned to the American continent. Since then he has taught at a variety of universities from Manitoba to Florida, including Princeton and Emory. In 1959, as a Fulbright Professor at the Centre d'Études Supérieures de la Renaissance in Tours he ranged from Algiers to Tours as a visiting lecturer. He is now a Professor of English in the Graduate School of New York University.

Bibliographical Series
of Supplements to 'British Book News'
on Writers and Their Work

GENERAL EDITOR
Bonamy Dobrée

FRANCIS BACON

from the studio of Paul van Somer
National Portrait Gallery

FRANCIS BACON

by

J. MAX PATRICK

> . . . I have, and do reverence him for the greatness that was only proper to himself, in that he seemed to me ever, by his work, one of the greatest men, and most worthy of admiration, that had been in many ages. In his adversity I ever prayed that God would give him strength: for *greatness* he could not want.
>
> Ben Jonson, *Discoveries*, 1641

PUBLISHED FOR
THE BRITISH COUNCIL
and the NATIONAL BOOK LEAGUE
by LONGMANS, GREEN & CO.

LONGMANS, GREEN & CO. LTD.
6 & 7 Clifford Street, London W.1
Thibault House, Thibault Square, Cape Town
605–611 Lonsdale Street, Melbourne, C.1.

LONGMANS, GREEN & CO. INC.
119 West 40th Street, New York 18

LONGMANS, GREEN & CO.
20 Cranfield Road, Toronto 16

ORIENT LONGMANS PRIVATE LTD.
Calcutta   Bombay   Madras
Delhi   Hyderabad   Dacca

Printed in Great Britain by
F. Mildner & Sons, London, E.C.1

CONTENTS

¶ Francis Bacon was born on 22 January, 1561, in London. He died on 9 April, 1626

FRANCIS BACON

I

FRANCIS BACON, BARON VERULAM OF VERULAM, VISCOUNT
ST. ALBANS (1561–1626) flourished in an age of paradoxes,
violent contrasts, and sudden reversals. In it, more
markedly than in other periods, the whirl of Fortune's
wheel tossed men to summits of fame and power and cast
illustrious leaders down to ignominy or death. It was an age
which revelled in gorgeous façades, splendour, and display,
masques, metamorphoses, and triumphal processions, a time
of extraordinary virtuosity and versatility. Bacon's career
and works manifest the rich baroque diversity of his times,
not typically but in a heightened degree. In him were mixed
greatness and pettiness, magnanimity and craftiness; and his
life was punctuated by sudden dislocations and reversals of
policy, position, and wealth. After long delay and frustra-
tion, he soared to rank and power and balanced on the
slippery pinnacle of judicial office for eight years, only to be
precipitated into disgrace and retirement at the very moment
when he seemed most secure.

Bacon's zest for grandeur was colossal, but he also
cherished reading 'in privateness and retiring' and savoured
gardening as 'the purest of human pleasures'. Most of his
works begin as splendid façades, and some of them consist
of little more than a front of vast promises, dedications,
introductions, and preliminaries. But his range as an author
also extended to long treatises and brief essays. Though his
life glittered with costly stores of fine raiment, grand
mansions, vast staffs of liveried servants, and superb cere-
monials, he also found contentment in retreating to the
relative simplicity of his rooms in Gray's Inn. Since he
lived extravagantly, his debts and generosity were as grand
as his tastes and talents.

Above all, he was endowed with suppleness of mind, virtuosity which has few parallels, and universality of interests. He is the supreme English exemplar of the Baroque Man, a master of the traditions and methods of the past, able to exploit or surpass or vary them with adroit dislocations, reversals, and twistings—in short, with the incredibly flexible technique of a baroque artist. Though his career and ideas fell into a pattern, they were constantly shifting focus and undergoing transformations, resembling the metamorphoses in the court masques of his time. His goal was power for grand ends and philanthropic glory. He won both, and contempt as well. Like baroque art, he embraced a dialectic of opposites and extremes and a vastness of scope which intricated the sacred and the secular, the sublime and the sordid, the practical and the ideal, and somehow involved them all in precarious balance.

II

Francis was born on 22 January, 1561, which enabled him as a child to flatter Queen Elizabeth by stating his age as 'just two years younger than your Majesty's happy reign'. In return, she called him her 'young Lord Keeper' in reference to his father, Sir Nicholas Bacon, Lord Keeper of the Great Seal. Francis later described him as 'plain, direct, and constant, without . . . doubleness'. Lady Ann, his second wife, was the erudite but exacting daughter of Edward VI's tutor. She was 'exquisitely skilled in the Greek and Latin tongues', firm in character, and resolutely Calvinist in religion. Her influence upon her elder son, Antony, and upon Francis can hardly be overestimated. From her the latter probably derived his energy, his discursiveness, and his seriousness of purpose. At his request, he was buried in the same church with her.

At the age of twelve, Francis entered Trinity College,

Cambridge, and four years later was admitted to Gray's Inn to study law. In 1577 he joined the suite of Elizabeth's Ambassador to France and remained there until his father's sudden death brought him home in his eighteenth year to a 'narrow portion' and the necessity of earning his own living in the ruthlessly competitive society and court of Elizabethan London.

Ambition, awareness of his abilities, and the reasonable hope that his maternal relatives, the influential Cecils, would be helpful, led him to solicit his uncle, Lord Burleigh, for public office. But neither Elizabeth's chief minister nor the Queen herself encouraged him. In the essay 'Of Great Place', Bacon later reflected on the obsession for eminence which then afflicted him:

> It is a strange desire, to seek power and lose liberty, or to seek power over others and to lose power over a man's self. The rising unto place is laborious, and by pains men come to greater pains, and it is sometimes base; and by indignities men come to dignities. The standing is slippery, and the regress is either a downfall or at least an eclipse, which is a melancholy thing.

When Bacon wrote these musings he had learned to regret the sycophancy and scheming involved in his rise. In 1584 he entered Parliament, and in 1603 James created him a knight. But almost three years of fawning and striving elapsed before, in his middle age, he became Solicitor-General in 1607. Six years later he was inducted as Attorney-General, and in 1617–18 became Lord Keeper, Lord Chancellor, and Baron Verulam. Though the title of Lord St. Alban was added in 1621, he is known to history simply as Francis Bacon.

Originally his avowed goals were of the highest order. When about twenty-three, he composed *The Greatest Birth of Time, or the Great Renewal of the Empire of Man over the Universe* to announce a new method of scientific discovery which would show his countrymen how to use nature 'for the glory of God and the use of man's estate.' 'I confess', he wrote to his uncle, 'that I have as vast contemplative ends as I have moderate civic ends, for I have taken all knowledge to be my province.' And in the *Essays* Bacon made noble acknowledgments:

> Merit and good works is the end of man's motion . . .
> . . . truth, which only doth judge itself, teacheth that the inquiry of truth (which is the love-making or wooing of it), the knowledge of truth (which is the presence of it), and the belief of truth (which is the enjoying of it), is the sovereign good of human nature.

In his thirtieth year Bacon met the Queen's favourite, the Earl of Essex:

> I held at that time my Lord to be the fittest instrument to do good in the state, and therefore I applied myself to him in a manner which rarely happeneth among men.

Since court business tended to flow through the hands of the favourite, Essex had need of a shrewd adviser and capable administrative helper. Bacon's industry and experience proved so useful that his patron tried to reciprocate by opening high public office to him. But the Queen resisted the Earl's tactless overtures for the advancement of his henchman, and in the end Bacon was generously repaid with one of his lordship's valuable estates. However, when the impetuous aristocrat ignored his counsellor's warnings and imperilled his Queen and country by drifting into treasonable activities, thus making his own ruin certain, Bacon testified against him and helped to prosecute him for treason; he did so with a vigour which suggests that the bond between them had been an irksome one based on mutual convenience. The result was death for the popular Earl and the blackening of Bacon's reputation by charges that he was a sort of Judas.

Bacon's unflagging loyalty to Tobie Matthew may be put in the balance against this callous treatment of Essex. When Matthew, son of the Archbishop of Canterbury, scandalized Protestant England by becoming a Roman Catholic, Bacon effected his release from prison and received him into his home while the convert prepared to go into banishment. Despite the anti-Romanist pressures engendered by the Gunpowder Plot, their friendship persisted and Matthew paid fine tribute to it after Bacon's death:

> It is not his greatness that I admire, but his virtue; it is not the favours I have received from him (infinite though they be) that have thus enthralled and enchained my heart, but his whole life and character.

Bacon and his closest associates were mutually loyal. 'He and his servants had all in common', observed Thomas Fuller. His relations with his brother Antony were ever harmonious. According to Peter Boener, Bacon's apothecary, he was 'a noteworthy example and pattern for everyone of virtue, gentleness, peacefulness, and patience'. He was able to refer to George Herbert, John Selden, Thomas Hobbes, and other men who assisted him in his writings as 'good pens that do not forsake'. And his chaplain, Dr. Rawley, noted that Bacon was 'much revered and beloved at Gray's Inn':

> . . . he was no dashing man as some men are, but ever a countenancer and fosterer of another man's parts. Neither was he one that would appropriate the speech wholly to himself, or delight to outvie others, but leave a liberty to the co-assessors to take their turns. . . . He condemned no man's observations, but would light his torch at every man's candle.

When James I ascended to the throne in 1603, Bacon hoped that the erudite monarch would further the vast schemes which he set forth in the *Advancement of Learning*, but petitions, flattery, and the great treatise itself failed to win royal support for Bacon's philosophical programme. 'The King', it was maliciously reported, 'cannot forbear sometimes in reading his last book to say that it is like the peace of God that passeth all understanding'. But James recognizing Bacon's other talents and, pleased by his pliancy and obsequiousness, advanced him to high offices and honours, though he failed to save him in 1621 when a rival political faction forced him from power. For all his sagacity Bacon had fallen into debt and had accepted gifts, some of them from suitors in cases which he was trying in the courts. The receiving of such 'benefactions' by men of influence, though contrary to the letter of the law, was an expected part of the fruits of office. 'If I were . . . to punish those who take bribes,' King James told the Ambassador from Venice, 'I should soon not have a single subject left'. So prevalent was the practice that Bacon made little or no effort at concealment: 'Strange to me', commented his chief enemy Lord Coke, 'that this money should be thus openly delivered'. It might be argued that the presents, though intended as bribes, were not received as such by Bacon, for most of the bribers who gave evidence against him had received adverse decisions from him. In any case, he was always candid about distinguishing between the absolute ethics of theory and the compromising morality of practice. Neither he nor his attackers emulated the integrity of his saintly predecessor in the Lord Chancellorship, Sir Thomas More. Those who denounce Bacon seem chiefly disturbed by the frankness of his observations made in the *Essays*:

> . . . mixture of falsehood is like alloy in coin of gold or silver, which may make the metal work the better . . .

If a man is to keep a secret, he must give himself 'a little scope for dissimulation'. Practical men gain a reputation for honesty, but practise 'secrecy in habit, dissimulation in seasonable use, and a power to feign, if there be no remedy'.

When Bacon was charged with accepting bribes, the King urged him to make no defence. Accordingly he was convicted on his own confession, fined £40,000, excluded from public office, and sentenced to imprisonment at the royal pleasure. He was almost immediately freed; the fine was made over to his debtors; and he received a full pardon in 1624. But he learned that 'there is no vice that doth so cover a man with shame as to be found false and perfidious'.

Though Bacon was sixty, and an indefatigably active life entitled him to leisure, his restless mind allowed him no idleness. In vain he kept trying to re-enter public life; and in the meantime he returned to the grand design for the advancement of science which he had nourished from his youth.

Despite his prodigious busyness as jurist, parliamentarian, and councillor, he had already managed to publish *The Colours of Good and Evil*, on the art of persuasion, along with the first edition of his *Essays* in 1597; the latter appeared in enlarged form in 1612 and reached completion in 1625. He also published *The Advancement of Learning Divine and Humane* (1605), *De Sapientia Veterum*, Of the Wisdom of the Ancients (1609), and *Instauratio Magna*, The Great Instauration (1620), alternatively titled *Novum Organum*, The New Organon. In addition he composed *Maxims of the Law* (1596) and numerous other professional works on Essex's treason, controversies in the Church, the union of England and Scotland, the plantation of Ireland, and the like. Now, in retirement, he turned to writing, the pursuit of science, and the pleasures of gardening.

'God Almighty first planted a garden'. Such is the typically striking beginning of the essay on gardening, 'the greatest refreshment to the spirits of man'. Bacon probably wrote those words in his rooms at Gray's Inn. Late in the 1590's he and a friend had transformed the grounds of the Inn into a little park. They first planted elms and a quickset hedge and later added eight birches, sixteen cherry trees, over a hundred standards of roses, a variety of flowers which included pinks, violets, and primroses, and also, according to legend, a catalpa tree presented by Sir Walter Raleigh.

According to Bacon's chaplain, his extravagance in money was offset by his allowing 'no moment nor fragment of time to pass away unprofitably'. 'Of Gardens' reveals that the profit he sought was by no means confined to the utilitarian, for Bacon cared about little things: 'violets, especially the single blue, which are the earliest', 'the pale daffodil, the French honeysuckle, the cherry-tree in blossom, the damson and plum-trees in blossom, the white thorn in leaf, the lilac-tree'. He remarks that roses are retentive of their fragrance, 'so that you may walk by a whole row of them and find nothing in their sweetness, yea, though it be in the morning's dew'; on the other hand, 'That which above all others yields the sweetest smell in the air is the violet, specially the white double violet, which comes twice a year, about the middle of April and about Bartholomew-tide. Next to that is the musk-rose. Then the strawberry-leaves dying, with a most excellent cordial smell.'

This mild aspect of Bacon extended to offenders tried in his courts. According to Rawley:

> he was never of an insulting or domineering nature over them, but always tender-hearted . . . as one that looketh upon the example with the eye of severity, but upon the person with an eye of pity and compassion.

Such a kindly attitude was proper to one who held the high ideal of service which he expressed about 1603 in the Latin proem to an intended work on the interpretation of nature:

> Believing that I was born for the service of mankind, and regarding the care of the commonwealth as a kind of common property which, like the air and the water, belongs to everybody, I set myself to consider in what way mankind might be best served, and what service I was myself best fitted by nature to perform.

He decided that he was 'fitted for nothing so well as for the study of Truth.' Though distracted from this noble pursuit

by his own worldly ambitions, and baffled by his failure to
win royal backing for his grand design, and by his seeming
inability to secure a strong group of followers who would
further it, Bacon never grew misanthropical. Even after his
disgrace, it was in a resolutely optimistic spirit that he composed a biography of Henry VII (1622) and a Latin expan-
sion of the *Advancement* entitled *De Augmentis Scientiarum*
(1623). He also dictated a book of *Apophthegms* and left for
posthumous printing *Sylva Sylvarum, or a Natural History*,
and the unfinished *New Atlantis* (1626–27). After his death
on 9 April, 1626, the historian William Camden summed
him up as follows:

> He was of a middling stature; his countenance had indented with
> age before he was old; his presence grave and comely; of a high-
> flying and lively wit, striving in some things to be rather admired
> than understood; yet so quick and easy where he would express
> himself, and his memory so strong and active, that he appeared the
> master of a large and plenteous storehouse of knowledge, being (as
> it were) Nature's midwife, stripping her callow brood, and clothing
> them in new attire. His wit was quick to the last. . . . In fine, he
> was a fit jewel to have beautified and adorned a flourishing King-
> dom, if his flaws had not disgraced the lustre that should have set
> him off.

III

Prudence, the art of getting on in the world, was the
main theme of the ten brief essays which Bacon published
in 1597; he compared them to halfpennies: 'though the
silver were good, yet the pieces were small.' These 'frag-
ments', as he termed them, are groupings of pithy sayings
and maxims slightly expanded from a commonplace book.
Such collections of noteworthy passages were frequently
made by Elizabethans and were the forerunners of the formal
essay. For example, the anonymous *Remedies against Dis-
contentment* (1596) contained 'small discourses' on dis-
sembling and vanity. The Baconian essay of 1597 consisted

of a string of incipient paragraphs related to a subject such
as Studies, Discourse, Suitors, Expense, Faction, and Nego-
tiating. The expression was terse and aphoristic, each little
division being independent of the others structurally. In
them Bacon favours lists of three: 'Reading maketh a full
man, conference a ready man, and writing an exact man.'
Sometimes he develops this triplicity in a parallel sentence:

> Studies serve for pastimes, for ornaments, and for abilities. Their
> chief use for pastime is in privateness and retiring; for ornamenta-
> tion is in discourse; and for ability is in judgement.

The weightiness of these threes is often relieved by pairings
or antitheses: 'They perfect Nature and are perfected by
experience.' More complexly, antitheses may be ranged in
a compressed triple series, as in 'Histories make men wise,
poets witty; the mathematics subtle; natural philosophy
deep, moral grave; logic and rhetoric able to contend.'
Such a passage momentarily halts the reader, forcing him
to fill out the hiatuses in order to grasp the meaning that
poets make men witty, mathematics make them subtle,
natural philosophy makes them deep, moral philosophy
makes them grave, etc. This device of compelling the reader
to think, along with the symmetry of the paired and triple
constructions and their parallels and antitheses, makes the
statements memorable. They give a sense of deep sagacity.
Actually, they usually state not the profound, but the
obvious. For example, in the 1625 edition of the *Essays*, the
revised 'Of Studies' began as follows:

> Studies serve for delight, for ornament, and for ability. Their
> chief use for delight is in privateness and retiring, for ornament is
> in discourse, and for ability is in the judgment and disposition of
> business.

This is an obvious improvement on the earlier wording
quoted above, and it is certainly impressive. But the meaning is almost trite and the compression does not achieve
brevity; for Bacon could have written: We read books to

please ourselves when we are alone, to impress others in conversation, and to improve our judgement and efficiency in practical affairs. What he achieves is an elevation of the familiar. He gives it dignity and significance, engraving it upon the mind, to be remembered because of its aptness and perfect wording.

Between 1607 and 1612 Bacon added twenty-four essays to revisions of the earlier ones but did not publish them in that form. In the intended prefatory letter he called them: 'Certain brief notes set down rather significantly than curiously, which I have called *Essays*'. The term, which means a trial, tentative effort, or assay, was borrowed from Montaigne. The Frenchman's essays were informal, self-revealing, and discursive; Bacon's are of a different type, impersonal, brief, and descriptive.

In the second edition (1612), the essays were enlarged 'both in number and weight', according to Bacon, 'so that they are indeed a new work', and 'come home to men's business and bosoms'. Twenty-nine new topics such as Religion, Death, Empire, and Fortune were introduced under the descriptive title, *Essays, or Counsels Civil and Moral*, and the style was made more periodic.

The style in the fifty-seven essays of the final edition (1625) is even less contracted. Transitions are eased, coherence is improved, and illustrative material is inserted. But the fact that the sentences tend to be longer, more fluid, and more closely interrelated does not justify a view that Bacon gradually learned to write in this 'literary' manner. He was a master of numerous and varied styles throughout his writing career. The abrupt, runic style of the earlier essays was a deliberate choice.

In the essays Bacon's usual method is to weigh and balance matters, indicating the ideal course of action and the practical one, pointing out the advantages and disadvantages of each, but leaving the reader to make the final decisions. Since his purpose is not the expression of his own feelings, it is inappropriate to approach the essays like a Romantic critic in search of an author's revelation of himself, just as it is anachronistic to judge Bacon's career by the yardstick of Victorian morality. The essays on marriage, children, and single life alternate between arguments in their favour and arguments in their disfavour without committing him certainly to either side. As his other works reveal, he was not lacking in egotism and exhibitionism, but what he made public in the essays was not an introspective probing of his private being but a *persona*, a public role which he assumed. He puts on the mask of a sagacious, hard-headed counsellor who is aware of the ways of the world and not afraid to point out what will accord with them. He describes how men succeed in competitive society. The enjoyment of truth may be the 'sovereign good of human nature', but, having acknowledged that fact, he passes to 'the truth of civil business', the facts about what men do in ordinary affairs where 'the mixture of a lie' is sometimes effective. It is 'holy and religious' to meditate upon death, but obsessive fear of dying impedes a man's efficiency. 'Revenge is a kind of wild justice', but it is best left to the law or nobly neglected, for it distracts a man's time and energy from the advancement of his career. Adversity is unpleasant to endure, but practical people learn fortitude from it and thus gain strength to move on to success. A wife and children may be impediments to great enterprises, but they are a discipline to humanity and may curb a husband and father from harmful endeavours. The envy of others is often dangerous to a man in high position, but clever man avoids its ill effects by managing things so that the envy is transferred to someone else, such as his dependents or associates. (No wonder that William Blake called the essays 'good advice for Satan's Kingdom!'). Love is all right for the stage, 'but in life it doth much mischief', especially in its 'mad degree'; therefore 'men ought to beware of this passion' and, 'if they cannot but admit love', they will 'do best' to 'sever it wholly from their serious affairs and actions of life'. In such passages Bacon sees that men are mixtures of good and bad and accepts them as such. A reader should approach him in the same manner. Certainly, to interpret him romantically as a disappointed idealist is to misunderstand his nature and intentions. His essays, like his whole philosophical system, are rooted in realistic observations of facts. Though he may sometimes seem cynical in his appraisal of those facts, it should be remembered that his estimate of them led him to optimism.

IV

Bacon's optimism was persistent. It was easy to be hopeful during the glorious part of Queen Elizabeth's reign when, in his words, England had enjoyed 'continuance' or stability, general good health, peace, plenty, wealth, and reasonable prices for goods: many new houses were being erected, and there were 'the like pleasures of goodly gardens and orchards, walks, pools, and parks . . . beautiful and costly tombs and monuments . . . all sorts of grounds for fencing, manuring, and all sorts of good husbandry . . . towns never better built . . . rivers cut by hand and brought into a new channel; . . . so many excellent artificers . . . new handicrafts . . . new commodities made within the realm . . . such complete and honourable provision of horse, armour, weapon, ordinance of war', increased population, purity of religion and coinage, and a mighty navy.

Since Bacon was writing for propagandist purposes in this portion of *Certain Observations upon a Libel* (1592), he indulged in some exaggeration, omitting to mention the problem of increasing poverty, for example. Indeed, the account reads like an anticipation of his utopian New Atlantis; but it was not unjustified.

England in the later Elizabethan and Jacobean period was less happy. It was racked by changes in ideas, politics, and society which were revolutionary in pace. But Bacon, unlike some of his contempories, did not succumb to the disease of melancholy which Robert Burton anatomized; nor did he whine about 'all coherence gone' or complain that 'new philosophy calls all in doubt'. Bacon was not ignorant of the economic and social defects of his time, the prevalence of corruptions in government and law, the rising tensions which ultimately led to the Civil War. But he also saw the fact that England and Scotland were essentially and potentially good.

A significant instance of this optimism is to be found in the essay 'Of Plantations'. Other writers in the seventeenth and eighteenth centuries were prone to praise savages as noble and to use their reactions to European civilization as a vehicle for denouncing its weaknesses. In contrast, Bacon reverses this approach, urging that natives from overseas should be brought to England 'that they may see a better condition than their own and commend it when they return'.

Bacon was one of the first thinkers to accept and popularize the idea of progress. Unlike many men of his period, he would not dismiss defects in society and knowledge as God's will, or as the unavoidable results of human depravity and God's curse after the sin of Adam and Eve. Nor would he subscribe to the prevalent doctrine that nature was decaying. In the changing circumstances and ideas of his time, Bacon saw opporunity, not reason for despair. In his opinion there was need for an efficient and systematic appraisal of man's achievements and of the obstacles which stood in the way of further advances. Based on this appraisal, there should be a programme to promote learning and speed progress. Knowledge meant power, and power meant the empire of man over himself and nature. To these ends Bacon propounded his grand design:

> Francis of Verulam reasoned thus with himself, and judged it to be for the interest of the present and future generations that they be made acquainted with his thoughts.

Such is the beginning of his *Instauratio Magna*, *The Great Renewal of Learning* (1620):

> . . . he thought all trial should be made, whether that commerce between the mind and the nature of things, which is more precious than anything on earth, or at least anything that is of the earth, might by any means be restored to its perfect and original condition, or, if that may not be, yet reduced to a better condition than that in which it now is.

To this end Bacon would 'commence a total reconstruction of the sciences, arts, and all human knowledge raised upon the proper foundation'.

This Great Instauration was to have six main parts. Some of the works which Bacon had already published could be fitted into it; others which he was yet to compose would complement them; the rest would have to be filled in by others:

> The first part exhibits a summary or general description of the knowledge which the human race at present possesses . . . not only things already invented and known, but likewise omitted which ought to be there.

In large measure Bacon accomplished these aims in the *Advancement* and its Latin redaction, *De Augmentis*. In them he defends learning against its detractors, urges rulers to patronize it, and divides it into two kinds, the divine and the human, warning men 'that they do not unwisely mingle or confound these learnings together'.

This separation of natural science from divinity was one of Bacon's most important doctrines, for science had been subordinated to theology and partly stifled by it. The difficult problem of how spiritual things are related to natural ones was involved. In theology, what is called the Level of Nature includes everything which may be known to a pagan who lacks the revelations of the Hebrew-Christian God: thus More's Utopians, who are in a state of nature, have knowledge of natural law, natural philosophy, natural science, and natural theology. Though they lack revealed

truths, they are aware that there is a God and that laws
govern the universe, ethics, politics, etc. Unknown to them
is the Level of Grace or Spirit, which includes sacred
mysteries, theology, the divinely ordained institution of the
Church, and the like.

Various theories have been offered about the relationship
between the Levels of Grace and Nature. Utter materialists
deny the former; idealists tend to deny the latter. Bishop
Berkeley in the eighteenth century argued that the two
areas were separate but that God's fiat made one correspond
to the other, so that spirit seemed to act on matter and *vice-
versa*. Some austerely pious men believed that the Level of
Nature should be repudiated as far as possible and therefore
condemned the pagan philosophies of the Ancient Greeks,
the secular drama of Shakespeare, and the beauties of secular
music. As a Christian Humanist, John Milton refrained from
such repudiation and held that whatever is truly good on
the Level of Nature conduces to truth on the Level of Grace,
that the one merges into the other, that Platonic philosophy,
for example, groped toward the higher truths of Christianity and conduced to them. But Bacon propounded what
theologians call the Principle of Segregation, namely, that
there are two quite distinct realms of truth which are irrele-
vant to each other and must be kept in separate compart-
ments. Thus truth on the Level of Grace may state that the
world was created by divine commands in six days and that
the sun revolves around the earth. But the truth discovered
on the Level of Nature may be that creation was evolu-
tionary and that the earth revolves around the sun. By
segregating such truths, Bacon helped to free science from
the trammels of divinity; the examples given are not his,
however. He did not deny that in the long run spiritual
truth mattered most. But in the meantime, natural truth
might be made practically valuable.

Bacon does not hold to the principle of segregation con-
sistently throughout his works. At times he was closer to the
Christian Humanist position. But it is folly to expect com-

plete consistency in his teachings. In this respect they
resemble the thought of Plato, who did not hesitate to
assume different positions in different works, attacking
poetry and music in his Republic but exalting them in
some of his dialogues, for example. Bacon is consistent in
his goals of seeking to advance knowledge and men's con-
sequent empire over nature, but he willingly explores
different approaches to truth and changes his mind or varies
his programme to suit different times, audiences, and purposes. Most of his writings are subordinated to immediate
persuasive efficacy. Thus when he wrote the *Advancement*,
he formulated it in English for Protestant readers and took
advantage of their anti-Romanism to convince them. But
when he rewrote the work in Latin for a European audience,
he expunged his censures of Roman Catholicism.

In the *Advancement* and *De Augmentis* Bacon defends
Learning as if she were a client on trial before the bar of
public opinion—a technique which Sir Philip Sidney had
used in apologizing for poetry. Bacon begins by clearing
Learning's reputation from discrediting objections which
rose, he said, 'all from ignorance'. The impugners of
knowledge pointed to Solomon's warning that it increased
anxiety and to St. Paul's caveat against vain philosophy;
and they alleged that lust for knowledge caused the Fall of
Man and that learned times inclined to atheism and heresy.
Bacon replied that these censures were inapplicable to 'the
pure knowledge of nature and universality' and could be
directed only against 'the proud knowledge of good and
evil', that is, against man's efforts 'to give a law unto himself, and to depend no more upon God's commandments'.
Though science was to be pursued independently of
theology, both were important. Moreover, the learning
which Bacon advocated is mixed with the 'corrective spice'
of Charity: it is directed to the good of mankind and is
subject to three limitations. We must not 'so place our
felicity in knowledge, as to forget our mortality'. We must
apply our learning 'to give ourselves repose and content-

ment', not to make ourselves unhappy and restless; and we must not delude ourselves that by contemplating nature we may attain the mysteries of God.

Milton was to echo something of this passage near the end of *Paradise Lost*. Adam, having learned how 'one greater Man' would 'restore us', remarks on the contentment which this truth gives him and indicates the proper limits of knowledge:

> Greatly instructed I shall hence depart,
> Greatly in peace of thought, and have my fill
> Of knowledge, what this vessel can contain;
> Beyond which was my folly to aspire.

He has learned to obey God and depend upon Him. The Archangel approves, and tells Adam to hope for no higher wisdom: knowledge of 'all Nature's works/Or works of God', enjoyment of all worldly riches, and empire over them would not be superior. But the angel does not forbid mankind to gain this scientific knowledge: he insists on Bacon's proviso, the addition of deeds answerable to the knowledge, and of faith, virtue, patience, temperance, and love, 'By name to come call'd Charity, the soul/Of all the rest'.

Bacon similarly concludes this section of his argument by urging men to 'endeavour an endless progress or proficience' in both divinity and science: 'only let men beware that they apply both to charity and not to swelling [pride], to use and not to ostentation; and . . . that they do not unwisely mingle or confound these learnings together'.

V

'Having coasted past the ancient arts' in the first part of the Great Instauration, Bacon proceeded to his second point, 'to equip the intellect for passing beyond'. This task involved teaching men how to make 'better and more perfect use of human reason in the inquisition of things' and how to take advantage of 'the true helps of the understanding'. By such means the intellect could be 'raised and exalted and made capable of overcoming the difficulties and obscurities of nature'. Bacon attempted to fulfil these aims in his greatest philosophical work, The *New Organon, or Directions concerning the Interpretation of Nature*, which he wrote in Latin and revised twelve times before its publication in 1620. It was intended to replace Aristotle's Organon and to provide a new art of logic which would differ from Aristotle's 'in the end aimed at, in the order of demonstration, and in the starting point of the inquiry'. What the intellect needs, according to Bacon, is not the scholastic method of syllogisms, which only enables a man to win arguments, but a means to 'command nature in action', a form of induction which 'shall analyse experience and take it to pieces, and by due process of exclusion and rejection lead it to an inevitable conclusion'.

The reasoning used to 'prove' that the heavenly bodies are composed of a fifth essence, an element different from the four sublunary elements of earth, air, fire, and water, exemplifies what Bacon opposed:

> The heavenly bodies move eternally in circles. But it is the nature of earth and water to move down, and of air and fire to move up. Therefore the eternally circling heavenly bodies are not composed of earth, air, fire, and water, but of a fifth essence.

Such reasoning is valid if the first two propositions are true; Bacon objected that all too often they were assumptions based not on facts but on authority, tradition, novelty, prejudice, false reasoning, faulty observation, or inadequate evidence. He also objected that if the propositions were true they included the final statement and therefore merely clarified knowledge by bringing it into the open.

In his earliest works Bacon went to extremes in trying to avoid such unrealistic assumptions. He would draw up tables of facts and would narrow them by excluding what was not relevant. For example, in collecting facts about heat, he would learn that both dense and tenuous things could be hot; thus both denseness and tenuousness could be excluded from the possible forms of heat. In time, by means of such exclusions, he would arrive at an understanding of the real nature of heat.

In practice Bacon seems to have realized that tabulating and excluding were insufficient, for he began to advocate that researchers should sort out 'prerogative instances', facts which would be especially useful for gaining information or for indicating how to proceed. In other words, 'prerogative instances' would conduce to hypotheses—hypotheses which would then be tested by experiments, Bacon used to be called the father of experimental science, but his claim to this title was denied because his method of tables and exclusions is not the procedure of modern science whereby an experimenter somehow formulates a guess, tentative theory, or hypothesis and then tests it in experiments. However, if one reads between the lines and interprets Bacon with common sense, it is clear that he realized the impossibility of reaching final truth by means of tables and exclusions or from the 'axioms' or hypotheses which emerged from them. Hypothesizing inevitably was involved in the classifying, in the selection of prerogative instances, and in the formulation of the 'axioms'. Scientific truths would emerge when these were tested by systematic experiments.

Bacon's final method for research is given at the end of *New Atlantis:* first, all available information is gathered about experiments; to this is added what is discovered by men who 'try new experiments such as themselves think good'. The resulting information is then compiled and tabulated. Next, based on these collections and discussions about them, there are 'new experiments of a higher light, more penetrating into nature than the former'; and finally these latest discoveries by experiments are formulated 'into greater observations, axioms, and aphorisms'. Although Bacon did not clearly or fully state the method of hypothesis and verifications, it was implicit in such a system.

Certainly the experiment which caused his death, the stuffing of a chicken with snow to see if it would retard the spoiling, exemplifies the method of testing hypotheses by experiment.

The third part of the Great Instauration, a compendium of natural science entitled *The Phenomena of the World, or Natural and Experimental History for the Foundation of Philosophy or Science*, was only partially fulfilled by *Sylva Sylvarum*, a largely derivative compilation of a thousand statements about science and related subjects. The latter included information about witches, keeping oranges fresh, silencers for guns, the diseases of corn, the possibility of what is now called extra-sensory perception, and the significance of dreams. Bacon also planned to write six 'histories' for this third part of the Instauration and completed *The History of Winds*, *The History of Life and Death*, and part of The *History of Rarety and Density*.

The fourth part was realized only by an introduction, *The Ladder of the Understanding, or The Key to the Labyrinth;* in the main work Bacon intended to expose the workings of the mind from particular to general truths in the process of invention. The fifth part is represented only by *Precursors*, or *Anticipations of the Coming Philosophy*, in which he invites all men to record facts about nature and promises to show how much he had accomplished and how much others could accomplish by using common sense and ordinary proofs without employing his method. But conclusions so reached would be regarded as tentative. The last part of the Instauration, *The New Philosophy, or Active Science*, would replace such conclusions and would set forth the results of applying the new method to all the phenomena of the universe. Bacon left this section unwritten, as something beyond his powers.

Such was Bacon's Grand Design: most of it was left for posterity to realize, but some particular features of the works which he accomplished toward it deserve special comment.

VI

Bacon's positive idea of progress has its negative complement in iconoclasm directed against whatever impeded the advance of science. His famous doctrine of Idols illustrates this iconoclasm and the workings of his mind.

'Idols' is a term which he used figuratively for fallacies which block or distort men's perception of reality and their pursuit of truth. They are psychological barriers—prepossessions, prejudices, and delusions, emotional and sentimental biases. In short, they include all the imaginings which prevent men from seeing the object as it really is.

Bacon's concept of Idols did not develop at one time or in a step-by-step progression, but flexibly: in different works he shifted his emphases and classifications, discarding, exploring, and revising as he searched for the most accurate and most effective formulation of the doctrine; or perhaps it would be more just to state that he knew that no single systematization of words and ideas could perfectly describe and correspond to what he was trying to communicate. Moreover, it was typical of him to change and experiment with ideas and their arrangement. His theories undergo transformations kindred to the forms which fluctuate within a total pattern in Baroque art. Bacon imposes order on his ideas, but within his systems there is flux and movement suggestive of the spiralling found in Baroque architecture. Thus his ideas on Idols circle and rise and develop from work to work in a manner which might be diagrammed as a zigzag mounting within a spiral. In *The Male Birth of Time* (1593?), he mentions three kinds of Idols, those of the Theatre, Market-place, and Cave, and suggests another division between Idols of the Home and of the Highway, but gives no explanation of what they all mean. In *Valerius Terminus* (1585?), he gives a fourfold classification, substituting 'Palace' for 'Market-place' and adding Idols of the Nation or Tribe. But in the *Advancement* he reverts to a triple system and presents modified concepts of

Idols of the Tribe, Cave and Market-place, or Palace though he does not employ those terms; and in a marginal note, he divides Idols into the native and the adventitious. This last distinction was developed along with a new one in 1607, and the doctrine took other forms in later works before it reached its fullest description in the *New Organon*.

The following account will be confined to the most influential aspects of the doctrine regardless of its Protean variations.

Suppose that an ancient Greek philosopher's natural human tendency to connect and unify led him to mistake a man standing beside a horse for a creature with a human head and an equine body, that is, a centaur. Some of the philosopher's friends might believe his report because of his authority, others because of its novelty. Their accounts of the centaur might be read centuries later and accepted as true because of their antiquity, or because belief in the existence of centaurs had become common. Some profound mind might then argue from this instance that there must be like combination of man with bull or lion or elephant; and a philosopher might then formulate a principle of animal cohesion or a doctrine that the soul resides in the upper part of the human body.

These seven fallacies are examples of Idols. In the *Advancement* Bacon cautions against them:

> for the mind of man is far from the nature of a clear and equal glass, wherein the beams of things should reflect according to their true incidence; nay, it is rather like an enchanted glass, full of superstition and imposture, if it be not delivered and reduced.

Bacon stated in *Valerius Terminus* that he found in this enchanted glass 'four Idols or false appearances . . . every sort comprehending many divisions'. In *Novum Organum* he explained them in the following order:

Idols of the Tribe are mental characteristics common to all men such as the tendency to find order and regularity

where it is lacking (as in the instance of the Greek who
thought he saw a centaur), the proneness of men to, allow
their desire, pride, prejudice, hopes, and prepossessions to
blind them to realities; and men's inclination to trust their
five senses, despite their fallibility, without enlisting the
help of experiments:

Idols of the Cave are the fallacies imposed on individuals
by the limitations of their peculiar natures, environments,
and experiences. Each man lives in a world of his own, confined, as it were, to a cave, lacking reliable knowledge of
what exists outside it. As a result he is likely to see things
not as they are but distorted by his idiosyncracies and
specialties. Thus a musician may think that the soul is only
a harmony. In Bacon's opinion, William Gilbert, his contemporary, had overspecialized in the study of magnetism
to such a degree that he erred in trying to formulate a whole
philosophy in terms of it. Bacon therefore advised students
to hold in suspicion any idea which particularly appealed
to them:

'Idols of the Market place are the most troublesome of all'.
They are semantic fallacies, notions imposed on the mind
by words which 'entangle and pervert the judgement'. They
are either names of things which do not exist or inaccurate
and confused names for existent things. Of the former kind
are 'fictions which owe their origin to false and idle theories',
such as the notion that the goddess Fortune governs men's
destinies. Examples of distorting and ill-defined words are
not far to seek in the modern world of advertising and
doubletalk, when 'true democracy' has different meanings
in Russia, England, and Cuba, and a buyer is at a loss to
know what is meant by 'Guaranteed Pure' printed on a
label. Bacon concludes that 'It is not possible to divorce
ourselves from these fallacies and false appearances, because
they are so inseparable from our nature and condition of
life', but we must guard against them:

Idols of the Theatre are systems of dogma or philosophy
which have been invented with little or no regard to

realities: they resemble the fictions of stage plays which distract audiences from what *is* to illusory worlds. Such systems may be sophistical, extracting a great deal from a few facts, or empirical, extracting a little from many things, or superstitions, mixing philosophy with theology and tradition. All of these are errors because they do not see knowledge truly. The Sophists do not consult experience; the Empiricists are too easily satisfied; and the Superstitious contaminate knowledge and spread their fallacies widest of all. The Idols of the Theatre also influence the mind into excesses of dogmatism or denial.

Having discussed 'the several classes of Idols and their equipage', Bacon concludes that they must all 'be renounced and put away . . . and the understanding thoroughly freed and cleansed; the entrance into the Kingdom of Man, founded on the sciences, being not much other than the entrance into the Kingdom of Heaven, wherein none may enter except as a little child'.

Bacon's attack on Idols was timely and influential, and its effectiveness derived partly from the obvious validity of what he was saying and partly from the memorable and striking nature of the terms he used. However, he comes close to creating Idols himself, for the classification is rather arbitrary and can be confusing because its lines of demarcation are not clear. Our example of the fallacies which arose when the Greek imagined that he saw a centaur is not greatly illuminated if an effort is made to distribute them into Bacon's categories.

VII

Bacon's utopia, *New Atlantis, a Work Unfinished*, is the most immediately attractive of all his works. 'What a stupendous fabric of a College for Nature hath the great St. Albans reared!' exclaimed John Hall in 1646. It convinced

Peter Heylyn that Bacon surpassed Sir Thomas More 'in the excellency and sensibility of his intention', and in 1668 it elicited sympathetic praise from Joseph Glanvill: 'This great man desired and formed a society of experimenters in a romantic model but could do no more: his time was not ripe for such performances'. This use of 'romantic' is just: paradoxically, Bacon exploits imaginative fiction to advocate the scrupulous observance of scientific objectivity in well-organized co-operative research.

Though the presentation of the ideas was original, the ideas themselves were not. During Bacon's early visit to Paris, Bernard Palissy was urging the importance of experiments, collections of specimens, and teaching by means of practical demonstrations; and libraries and learned academies of various kinds had already been founded. Bacon had himself propounded most of the scheme in earlier works. His main non-scientific theme, glorification of the family as a stabilizing social factor in society was a commonplace. The importance of the utopia lies chiefly in the effectiveness with which ideas from a variety of sources were combined and given timely expression.

Bacon fired the imaginations of his readers. Instead of a cold Institute for Co-operative Scientific Research, he painted a romantic Solomon's House on the island-continent of a new Atlantis, thus associating his grand design with Solomon in his glory and wisdom, with the magnificence of the legendary civilisation described by Plato, and with the fascination of a mysterious island remote beyond uncharted seas. So Bacon roused his countrymen to awareness of the possibilities of co-operative research, applied science, and organized learning. His was the greatest influence in the creation of what is known as The Scientific Movement. The work of Palissy, Harvey, Gilbert, and most other scientists contemporary with Bacon was little noted by ordinary cultivated Englishmen, though Galileo was to some extent an exception. Bacon composed the *New Atlantis* in the vernacular so that it appealed to men of power and influence and to a still wider public of intelligent readers: he helped to focus their attention, their leisure time, and their unattached hopes upon science. He inspired those who would probably have ignored science to become gentlemen amateurs in it, to favour the Royal Society; and in time his writings made the whole western world conscious of the potentialities, achievements, and progress of science; he proved that utopianism need not be mere escapism; and the precedent of his own devotion to science gave it respectability and dignity.

Bacon's expectations for science have become commonplace, but the charm of his fiction remains a potent force. He sounded a bell for benefactors and thus promoted 'foundations and buildings, endowments with revenues . . . new editions of authors . . . and the reward and designation of writers and inquirers. . . .'

Bacon's chaplain, who saw *New Atlantis* through the press, prefaced it as follows:

> This Fable my Lord devised to the end that he might exhibit therein a model or description of a college instituted for the interpreting of nature and the producing of great and marvellous works for the benefit of men, under the name of Solomon's House, or the College of the Six Day's Works. . . . Certainly the model is more vast and high than can possibly be imitated in all things; notwithstanding, most things therein are within men's power to effect.

Obviously Bacon realized that his imaginary country could not be imitated in all respects: for example, its geography, history, and isolation could not be duplicated by Britain. As a matter of fact, relatively few utopias are intended to be literally copied: most of them are propounded not as goals of perfection but as norms by which readers can judge their own societies and discover some means of bettering them. It is ordinarily both foolish and futile to assume that the inventors of fictitious commonwealths believed them to be ideal or to waste time in searching for flaws and inconsistencies in their accounts. The question worth asking is: What features of this utopia are set forth as desirable and realisable?

The features of *New Atlantis* which Bacon hoped could be paralleled or approximated in England included respect for the dignity of the individual, calm courteousness in human relations and careful attention to hygiene, paternalism, piety, religious toleration, and reverence for the family; unfolded in this order, they take up three-quarters of the book. Their basis is the maximum utilization of available resources of men, ideas, and materials under the paternalistic guidance of men whose intelligences are disciplined and whose sense of moral and social responsibility has been highly developed. All this has been made possible in a capitalistic society by benevolent, state-supported scientific research and its results. But Bacon did not suffer from the delusion that the inventions which he lists near the end of the work—approximations or anticipations of telephones, submarines, aeroplanes and the like—would automatically bring about the moral and social regeneration of mankind. He did recognize that if men adhered to Christianity and to the best institutions and traditions of the past and also organized their talent so as to understand and control nature and themselves by means of science, in obedience to its laws, they would have prosperity and happiness, strength and health. Though he does not say so explicitly, he seems to have realized that materialistic achievement was not enough by itself: bathroom gadgets, automobiles, television sets, and atom bombs do not ensure happiness and decency. Bacon graphically showed that scientific and technological progress was desirable and practicable; but he devoted the major portion of *New Atlantis* to safeguards, preventives, and correctives which would prevent the intensive development and application of science from becoming a sort of Idol which would warp men's lives and thinking: hence his emphasis on the balancing and restraining factors—religion, home, philanthropy, responsibility, and charity. As he stated in the essay 'Of Truth', 'it is heaven upon earth to have a man's mind move in charity, rest in providence, and turn upon the poles of truth'. To enable man's mind to do so, his environment and attitudes had to be consciously changed by the responsible and judicious advancement of science in all its aspects in conjunction with an equally judicious retention of the tested ideas and institutions of the past.

VIII

Bacon's concern to do justice to the achievements of past generations extended to the advocacy of biographies. 'I do find it strange', he wrote in the *Advancement*,' . . . that the writing of lives should be no more frequent.' He commenced various studies of the Tudors and wrote brief sketches of Julius and Augustus Cæsar, but *The History of the Reign of King Henry the Seventh* was the only work in this genre which he brought to completion. He wrote it soon after his release from the Tower in 1621, partly to ingratiate himself with King James by immortalizing that monarch's grand-father, and partly because he regarded Henry VII as 'one of the most sufficient kings of all the number', as a ruler whose times deserved treatment and whose accomplish-ments merited recognition. 'For he was a wise man, and an excellent King.' Nevertheless, as Bacon pointed out in a prefatory letter, 'I have not flattered him, but took him to life as well as I could, sitting so far off and having no better light'.

Bacon did not delineate Henry VII as noble but as a dextrous politician who accomplished worthy goals and lacked magnanimity. The biography is couched in a con-tinued narrative which is felicitously phrased and illumin-ated by vivid details such as the story of how the royal monkey tore up the royal notebook. Though there is some over-attention to incidentals, the history is based on careful research; it is at once graced and marred by imaginary speeches put into the mouths of the characters. However, the explorations of the causes behind the events make the life a significant contribution to the rise of modern historiography.

Bacon was likewise concerned with his own reputation. 'I work for posterity', he wrote in 1625, and in his will he bequeathed his reputation 'to men's charitable speeches and to foreign nations and the next ages'.

Despite this apparent expectation that time would justify his ways to men, the controversies over his character, career, and ideas which chequered his reputation while he lived have persisted to the four hundredth anniversary of his birth in 1961. Though lauded by some as the greatest Englishman who ever lived, as a universal genius distinguished in law, politics, science, philosophy, and literature, he has been damned by others as a pseudo-scientist and corrupt judge who turned traitor to his talents as well as to his friend Essex, and gave to a self-centred career what was meant for mankind. In one respect alone, his importance has been unanimously recognized: in the history of English literature he is securely established as superb stylist, a great essayist, and a pioneer biographer, as a major contributor to the utopian genre, and as the author of a majestic treatise on the advancement of learning. But here lies an irony of fame: Bacon had no confidence in English as a medium for lasting communication. Though he resorted to it for immediate purposes, he preferred to compose his important works in Latin or to have them translated into what he called 'the universal language'. Such a Latin work, he thought, would 'live and be a citizen of the world as English books are not'. Yet his firmest reputation rests upon what he regarded as ephemeral writings in the vernacular and on the translations into it of his Latin masterpieces.

Bacon's outstanding characteristic was a virtuosity which his critics have variously termed 'marvellous versatility' and 'incomparable ductility'. It is discoverable even in his handwriting and is most remarkable in the infinite variety with which he adapts different styles of writing to different occasions, subjects, and readers. It reaches its nadir in the obsequious adeptness with which he moulded his talents to serve the wishes and the whims of kings, favourites, and men of influence. 'I am bold to think it, till you think otherwise', he wrote to Queen Elizabeth early in his career; and later in like manner, having expressed to Buckingham his dis-approval of some monopolies, he retreated into pliancy by adding, 'Howsoever, let me know your will, and I will go your way'.

Bacon could adjust himself to almost any role: he could be a Jonathan or a Judas to a friend, a sycophant or a ruthless enemy to a superior, an advocate of moderation or an ex-travagant exhibitionist. In such respects he differed from his seventeenth-century contempories more in degree than in nature. For they too were prone to assume personae and to live more richly with their masks than without them. Thus John Donne moved through the roles of poet-rake, scholar, and man of God; Ben Jonson lived as a romantic but wrote as a classicist; and Robert Burton found vitality when he cast off the don and became an imaginary Democritus Junior. Even men on trial for their lives or condemned to death acted out heroic roles with gusto. Bishop Andrews dramatised his sermons into artfully intense performances, and the Dean of St. Paul's found lugubrious satisfaction when he posed in his death shroud.

The assuming of such roles was not the result of insin-cerity but sprang from a genuine baroque impulse which led men to give themselves totally and fervently. The study of rhetoric trained students to throw themselves into assigned personae, to support either side of a controversial subject and to lend to it all their talents. Thus it is that Milton was able to identify himself with his Satan so dynamically that some readers of *Paradise Lost* have mistaken the devil for the hero of the epic.

Here then is the clue to Bacon's multiple sensibility, to

his inconsistencies and complexities. He tended to lose himself in the role of the moment. At its worst, this flexibility meant that he became all things to all men. At its best, it entitled him to John Aubrey's supremely felicitous tribute: 'All that were great and good loved and honoured him.'

FRANCIS BACON

A Select Bibliography

(Place of publication London, unless otherwise stated)

Bibliography:

FRANCIS BACON: A BIBLIOGRAPHY OF HIS WORKS AND OF BACONIANA TO THE YEAR 1750, by R. W. Gibson (1950).
— *Supplement*, 1959.

Collected Editions and Selections:

CERTAINE MISCELLANY WORKS (1629).

OPERUM MORALIUM ET CIVILIUM TOMUS (1638).

THE REMAINES BEING ESSAYES AND LETTERS AND OTHER PIECES (1648).
— reprinted, 1656, as *The Mirrour of State and Eloquence*.

SCRIPTA IN NATURALI ET UNIVERSALI PHILOSOPHIA, Amsterdam (1653).

RESUSCITATIO (1657, 1661, 1671).

OPUSCULA VARIA POSTHUMA (1658; Amsterdam, 1663).

BACONIANA, OR CERTAIN GENUINE REMAINS. Ed. T. Tenison (1679).

LETTERS WRITTEN DURING THE REIGN OF KING JAMES (1702).

LETTERS AND REMAINS (1734).

WORKS, edited by D. Mallet. 4 vols. (1740).

THE WORKS, edited by B. Montagu. 16 vols. (1825–36).

THE WORKS, edited by J. Spedding, R. L. Ellis and D. D. Heath. 7 vols. (1857–59).
— Vols. I–II, the Philosophical Works in Latin; IV–V, English translations of them; VI–VIII, Literary and Professional Works. The 7 vols. of Spedding's *The Letters and the Life* supplemented this edition with the Occasional Works and are sometimes numbered as vols. VIII–XIV.

THE PHILOSOPHICAL WORKS, reprinted from the Texts and Translations, with Notes and Prefaces of Ellis and Spedding, edited by J. W. Robertson (1905).

THE ADVANCEMENT OF LEARNING AND NEW ATLANTIS, preface by T. Case (1906).
—World's Classics.

SELECTIONS, WITH ESSAYS BY MACAULAY AND S. R. GARDINER, edited by P. E. and E. F. Matheson. Oxford (1922).
— Extracts from *Essays*, *Advancement*, *New Atlantis*, *Henry VII*.

ESSAYS, ADVANCEMENT OF LEARNING, NEW ATLANTIS, AND OTHER PIECES, edited by R. F. Jones. New York (1937).
— 'Odyssey Series', with introduction, notes and bibliography.

SELECTED WRITINGS, edited by H. G. Dick. New York (1955).
— Modern Library. The texts of *Essays, Clue to the Maze, Great Instauration, New Organon, New Atlantis:* extracts from the *Interpretation of Nature.*

Separate Works—Philosophical:

(a) *Parts of the INSTAURATIO MAGNA*

Novum Organum. INSTAURATIO MAGNA, PARS SECUNDA . . . NOVUM ORGANUM, SIVE INDICIA DE INTERPRETATIONE NATURAE (1620).
— ed. T. Fowler (Oxford, 1878; 2nd ed., 1889); Engl. trs. P. Shaw (1802); W. Wood (1844); G. W. Kitchin (1855); A. Johnson (1859); G. Kennedy (New York, 1937).
PARASCEVE AD HISTORIAM NATURALEM ET EXPERIMENTALEM (1620).
— tract appended to the *Novum Organum.*
DE AUGMENTIS SCIENTIARUM (1623).
— Pt. I of the *Instauratio;* an expanded Latin version of *The Advancement of Learning.* Eng. tr. G. Wats, Oxford, 1640.
Historia Ventorum. HISTORIA NATURALIS ET EXPERIMENTALIS AD CONDENDAM PHILOSOPHIAM: SIVE PHAENOMENA UNIVERSI (1622).
— *Instauratio* Pt. 3. Under this general title were published only *Historia Ventorum* and introductions to other 'Historiae'. Eng. tr. R. G. Gent, 1653.
HISTORIA VITAE ET MORTIS (1623).
— *Instauratio* Pt. 3. Eng. tr. W. Rawley, 1638.
HISTORIA DENSI ET RARI.
— intended for the *Instauratio* Pt. 3; first publ. in the collection *Operum moralium et civilium tomus primus,* 1638.
SYLVA SYLVARUM: OR A NATURALL HISTORIE (1627).
— intended for the *Instauratio* Pt. 3; publ. by W. Rawley with the *New Atlantis.* 10th ed. (1676) contains an epitome of *Novum Organum.*
SCALA INTELLECTUS, SIVE FILUM LABYRINTHI.
— intended for the *Instauratio* Pt. 4.
PRODROMI, SIVE ANTICIPATIONES PHILOSOPHIAE SECUNDAE.
— intended for the *Instauratio* Pt. 5.
Both the above tracts first publ. in the collection *Scripta in naturali et universali philosophia,* 1653.

(b) *Works connected with the INSTAURATIO but not intended to be included in it.*

NEW ATLANTIS (with *Sylva Sylvarum* 1627).
— ed. G. C. Moore Smith, Cambridge, 1900; A. B. Gough, Oxford, 1915.

COGITATIONES DE NATURA RERUM—DE FLUXU ET REFLUXU MARIS —DE PRINCIPIIS ATQUE ORIGINIBUS SECUNDUM FABULAS CUPIDINIS ET COELI.

— tracts first publ. in the collection *Scripta in naturali et universali philosophia*, 1653.

(c) *Works originally designed for parts of the INSTAURATIO but superseded or abandoned.*

THE TWOO BOOKES . . . OF THE PROFICIENCE AND ADVANCEMENT OF LEARNING (1605).

— ed. W. Aldis Wright, Oxford, 1869, rptd. in Clarendon Press Ser., 1900; F. G. Selby, 2 vols., 1893–5; G. W. Kitchin, in Everyman's Library, 1915; T. Case, with the *New Atlantis*, in the World's Classics, Oxford, 1906.

VALERIUS TERMINUS OF THE INTERPRETATION OF NATURE—PARTIS INSTAURATIONIS SECUNDAE DELINEATIO ET ARGUMENTUM ET REDARGUTIO PHILOSOPHIARUM—SEQUELA CARTARUM, SIVE INQUISITIO LEGITIMA DE CALORE ET FRIGORE.

— tracts first publ. in the collection *Letters and Remains*, 1734.

DE INTERPRETATIONE NATURAE PROOEMIUM—COGITATA ET VISA—FILUM LABYRINTHI, SIVE INQUISITIO LEGITIMA DE MOTO—DESCRIPTIO GLOBI INTELLECTUALIS—DE INTERPRETATIONE NATURAE SENTENTIAE DUODECIM—APHORISMI ET CONSILIA.

— tracts first publ. in the collection *Scripta in naturali et universali philosophia*, 1653.

HISTORIA ET INQUISITIO PRIMA DE SONO ET AUDITO.

— first publ. in the collection *Opuscula varia posthuma*, 1658.

Separate Works—Literary:

ESSAYES (1597).

— ten essays with 'Meditationes Sacrae' and 'Colours of Good and Evill'. Facs. eds. New York, 1904; Haslewood Books, 1924. Reprinted, 1612, with 38 essays, and 1625, with 58 essays. Ed. R. Whately, 1856; W. Aldis Wright, Cambridge, 1862; E. A. Abbott, 2 vols., 1876; S. H. Reynolds, 1890; R. Wright, 1924; G. Grigson, in the World's Classics, Oxford, 1937. *A Harmony of the Essays*, ed. E. Arber, 1871, enables comparison of the texts of 1597, 1612, and 1625. *Selected essays*, ed. J. Max Patrick, New York, 1948.

DE SAPIENTIA VETERUM (1609).

— Eng. tr. Sir A. Gorges, 1619.

THE HISTORIE OF THE REIGNE OF KING HENRY THE SEVENTH (1622).

— ed. J. R. Lumby, Cambridge, 1876.

OF THE TRUE GREATNESS OF THE KINGDOM OF BRITAIN.
— first publ. in the collection *Letters and Remains*, 1734.
APOPHTHEGMES NEW AND OLD (1625).
PROMUS OF FORMULARIES AND ELEGANCIES, BEING PRIVATE NOTES
　　CIRC. 1594. HITHERTO UNPUBLISHED (1883).
THE TRANSLATION OF CERTAINE PSALMES INTO ENGLISH VERSE (1625).
THE POEMS OF FRANCIS BACON. Ed. A. B. Grosart (1870).
— in vol. I of *Fuller's Worthies' Miscellany*.

Separate Works—Miscellaneous:

A DECLARATION OF THE PRACTICES & TREASONS ATTEMPTED AND
　　COMMITTED BY ROBERT, LATE EARLE OF ESSEX, AND HIS COMPLICES
　　(1601).
A BRIEFE DISCOURSE TOUCHING THE HAPPIE UNION OF THE KING-
　　DOMES OF ENGLAND AND SCOTLAND (1603).
CERTAINE CONSIDERATIONS TOUCHING THE BETTER PACIFICATION,
　　AND EDIFICATION OF THE CHURCH OF ENGLAND (1604).
APOLOGIE IN CERTAINE IMPUTATIONS CONCERNING THE LATE EARLE
　　OF ESSEX (1604).
CONSIDERATIONS TOUCHING A WARRE WITH SPAIN—AN ADVER-
　　TISEMENT TOUCHING AN HOLY WARRE—THE HISTORY OF THE
　　REIGNE OF KING HENRY THE EIGHTH.
— first publ. in the collection *Certain Miscellany Works*, 1629.
THE ELEMENTS OF THE COMMON LAWES OF ENGLAND, 2 pts. (1630).
THE CONFESSION OF FAITH (1641).
A WISE AND MODERATE DISCOURSE CONCERNING CHURCH AFFAIRS
　　(1641).
THE LEARNED READING . . . UPON THE STATUTE OF USES (1642).
THE FELICITY OF QUEEN ELIZABETH: AND HER TIMES (1651).
A CONFERENCE OF PLEASURE, COMPOSED FOR SOME FESTIVE OCCA-
　　SION ABOUT THE YEAR 1592. Ed. J. Spedding (1870).
REPORTS ON CASES DECIDED BY BACON IN THE COURT OF CHANCERY,
　　ed. J. Ritchie (1932).

Some Biographical and Critical Studies:

EXAMEN DE LA PHILOSOPHIE DE BACON, par J. M. de Maistre. Paris
　　(1836).
BACON, HIS LIFE AND PHILOSOPHY, by G. L. Craik (1846).
THE LETTERS AND LIFE OF FRANCIS BACON, INCLUDING ALL HIS
　　OCCASIONAL WORKS . . . WITH A COMMENTARY, BIOGRAPHICAL
　　AND HISTORICAL, by J. Spedding. 7 vols. (1861–74).
— abridged edition in one volume, 1878.
BACON, by T. Fowler (1881).

BACON, by R. W. Church (1884).
— in the English Men of Letters series.
FRANCIS BACON, HIS LIFE AND PHILOSOPHY, by J. Nichol. 2 vols. (1888–89).
MONTAIGNE ET BACON, par P. Villey. Paris (1913).
THE PHILOSOPHY OF FRANCIS BACON, by C. D. Broad. Cambridge (1926).
FRANCIS BACON, by A. E. Taylor (1926).
— a British Academy lecture.
FRANCIS BACON, THE POLITICAL ORATOR, by R. Hannah. New York (1926).
BACON, GILBERT, AND HARVEY, by W. H. White (1927).
'The Development of Bacon's Essays', by J. Zeitlin (1928).
— in Journal of English and Germanic Philosophy, XXVII.
SIR FRANCIS BACON, THE FIRST MODERN MIND, by 'B. Steel' [i.e., F. Steegmüller]. New York (1930).
FRANCIS BACON, A BIOGRAPHY, by M. Sturt. New York (1932).
BACON, by C. Williams (1933).
THE SEVENTEENTH-CENTURY BACKGROUND, by B. Willey (1934).
WIT AND RHETORIC IN THE RENAISSANCE, by R. S. Crane. New York (1937).
'Words for Princes', by G. Tillotson (1942).
— in Essays in Criticism and Research.
FRANCIS BACON ON COMMUNICATION AND RHETORIC, by K. R. Wallace. Chapel Hill (1943).
THE PHILOSOPHY OF FRANCIS BACON, by F. H. Anderson. Chicago (1948).
FRANCIS BACON: SA VIE, SON OEUVRE, par A. Cresson. Paris (1948).
FRANCIS BACON, PHILOSOPHER OF INDUSTRIAL SCIENCE, by B. Farrington. New York (1949).
THE SENECAN AMBLE, by G. Williamson (1951).
BACON: HIS LIFE AND WORKS, by A. W. Green. Denver (1952).
FRANCIS BACON, THE FIRST STATESMAN OF SCIENCE, by J. G. Crowther (1960).

WRITERS AND THIER WORK

General Editor: BONAMY DOBRÉE

The first 55 issues in the Series appeared under the
General Editorship of T. O. BEACHCROFT

Sixteenth Century and Earlier:
CHAUCER: Nevill Coghill
ENGLISH MARITIME WRITING:
 Hakluyt to Cook: Oliver Warner
MALORY: M. C. Bradbrook
MARLOWE: Philip Henderson
SIDNEY: Kenneth Muir
SKELTON: John Skelton
SPENSER: Rosemary Freeman

Seventeenth Century:
SIR THOMAS BROWNE: P. Green
BUNYAN: Henry Talon
CAVALIER POETS: Robin Skelton
DONNE: Frank Kermode
DRYDEN: Bonamy Dobrée
HOBBES: T. E. Jessop
BEN JOHNSON: J. B. Bamborough
ANDREW MARVELL: John Press
MILTON: E. M. W. Tillyard
SHAKESPEARE: C. J. Sisson
IZAAK WALTON: Margaret Bottrall
SHAKESPEARE:
   THE EARLY COMEDIES:
 Derek Traversi

Eighteenth Century:
BLAKE: Kathleen Raine
BOSWELL: P. A. W. Collins
BURKE: T. E. Utley
BURNS: David Daiches
COWPER: N. Nicholson
CRABBE: R. L. Brett
DEFOE: J. R. Sutherland
FIELDING: John Butt
GIBBON: C. V. Wedgwood
GOLDSMITH: A. Norman Jeffares
GRAY: R. W. Ketton-Cremer
HYMNS: Arthur Pollard
JOHNSON: S. C. Roberts
POPE: Ian Jack
RICHARDSON: R. F. Brissenden
SHERIDAN: W. A. Darlington

SMOLLETT: Laurence Brander
STEELE, ADDISON AND THEIR
 PERIODICAL ESSAYS:
       A. R. Humphreys
STERNE: D. W. Jefferson
SWIFT: J. Middleton Murry
HORACE WALPOLE: Hugh Honour

Nineteenth Century:
MATTHEW ARNOLD:
      Kenneth Allott
JANE AUSTEN: S. Townsend Warner
THE BRONTË SISTERS:
      Phyllis Bentley
BROWNING: John Bryson
SAMUEL BUTLER: G. D. H. Cole
BYRON: Herbert Read
CARLYLE: David Gascoyne
LEWIS CARROLL: Derek Hudson
COLERIDGE: Kathleen Raine
DICKENS: K. J. Fielding
GEORGE ELIOT: Lettice Cooper
ENGLISH TRAVELLERS IN THE
 NEAR EAST: Robin Fedden
FITZGERALD: Joanna Richardson
MRS. GASKELL: Miriam Allott
GISSING: A. C. Ward
THOMAS HARDY: R. A. Scott-James
HAZLITT: J. B. Priestley
G. M. HOPKINS: Geoffrey Grigson
T. H. HUXLEY: William Irvine
KEATS: Edmund Blunden
LAMB: Edmund Blunden
LANDOR: G. Rostrevor Hamilton
MACAULAY: G. R. Potter
JOHN STUART MILL: M. Cranston
WILLIAM MORRIS: P. Henderson
NEWMAN: J. M. Cameron
PATER: Iain Fletcher
ROSSETTI: Oswald Doughty
RUSKIN: Peter Quennell
SIR WALTER SCOTT: Ian Jack
SHELLEY: Stephen Spender